A high school janitor idly said "you could fatten a couple of pigs on the thrown-away lunches at this school" and a science project that gained recognition across Canada was born in West Vancouver.
Enjoy the antics of two engaging piglets in this first and only book by Ann Barker.

TAKE

A LUNCH TO PIG

A TRUE STORY

BY ANN BARKER

Order this book online at www.trafford.com
or email orders@trafford.com

Most Trafford titles are also available at major online book retailers.

Cover and page 1 sketch by MaryAnn Hager

Print information available on the last page.

ISBN: 978-1-4251-1246-2 (sc)

Trafford rev. 04/21/2023

Trafford PUBLISHING® **www.trafford.com**
North America & international
toll-free: 844-688-6899 (USA & Canada)
fax: 812 355 4082

WITH THANKS

To Tom, husband extraordinaire, for putting up with this story in our lives for 30 years.

To our children who always help out in these family adventures.

To Dave Urquhart and Jim Carter for the support given at school back then, as well as all the students who participated.

To Paul and Nicky Blakey who got me on the right track when writing started.

To Angeles at Trafford Publishing for her encouragement and expertise while I struggled with the manuscript.

To Gwen Hawkins, dear friend; great appreciation for her time, interest and encouragement in editing, rewriting and generously giving ideas in the right places.

To our daughter, MaryAnn for the wonderful cover sketch.

Articles reprinted with permission of Pacific Newspaper Group.

DEDICATION

For Tom

our children—
MaryAnn, Jane, Tom, Kim, John
with their partners

and our grandchildren—
Willis, Colton, Travis, Charlotte, Sam and Sol

You make the most wonderful family anyone could wish for.

WEST VANCOUVER SECONDARY SCHOOL

PIG PROJECT

WHAT IS IT?

Two pigs (two females - named Bert and Ernie) are being fattened by using the waste from our school lunch rooms.

WHY IS IT?

We wanted an integrated program that would give us an opportunity to publicize the problem of wasted food while at the same time being a benefit in our school setting. The project allows us to focus on:

- waste in school lunch areas.
- the value of recycling garbage.
- the study of pigs by senior biology students.
- the profit possible from creative use of waste.

WHO IS DOING IT?

The idea came from Mr. Kurt Kirmse, our head custodian. He has lamented the throwing away of perfectly good lunches for years. He made the fateful statement "We could fatten up a couple of pigs with what we throw out each day"!

The support for the idea came from :

- Mrs. Ann Barker, parent and member of the West Vancouver Secondary School Parent Advisory Committee. She thought up our slogan "Take a Lunch to Pig".

- Mr. Dave Urquhart, a senior biology teacher who saw the value in such a project for his students. He organized the following students as garbage collectors and pig tenders:

- PAUL GREENING	- TOM BARKER
- BRENDA MILLER	- CHRIS BRADLEY
- KAREN HALSTEAD	- JANE CRICKMORE

WHEN WILL THE PROJECT FINISH?

We hope to complete the project by the end of June. Some students have suggested they would like to enter the pair in the P.N.E.

FOREWORD

I have a story to tell you. It's not a long story but a story that is increasingly relevant as each day passes.

Thirty years ago, when we were inspired to do something about senseless waste by using it for a positive purpose, it was a case of "Let's do it!" "Let's show what can be done!" Each participant was full of energy and enthusiasm, ready to take on the little world.

Today, each is older and has a need to ration time and energy and the world is bigger, but the passion for ridding the world of waste remains a priority.

I've been waiting for just the right moment to tell this story. Increased awareness of our need to care for the environment, the increased waste in all sectors and THE YEAR OF THE PIG in Chinese astrology have all come together and met me at this point in time. Therefore, it seemed the auspicious moment to introduce you to some real home-grown heroes. As readers travel toward the story's inevitable conclusion, I hope many of you will recognize and act upon opportunities for making a difference in your personal lives and communities and that you receive joyous and satisfying rewards.

"Of all the sounds sounding
In this beautiful Earth dream
The one comes forth
To him who eavesdrops"

F. Schlegel

Take A Lunch To Pig

Walking down the hall of our high school one afternoon I saw my friend Kurt Kirmse, the janitor, leaning heavily on his broom while talking to a stranger. He looked worn and weary. As I got nearer, his words "you could fatten a couple of pigs" caught my ear. I didn't know how these simple words would soon affect my life, my family, the lives of other people, and a couple of adorable little animals, but affect us they did.

Stopping to find car keys in my pocket, I clearly overheard him lamenting about the amount of wasted food in the cafeteria. It was the number of unopened lunch bags being tossed into the garbage that bothered him. He was an angry man. He was disgusted with the thoughtlessness of some students. I was intentionally eavesdropping now, as I heard him say, "But it's nothing new. They've been throwing food away for a long time. I've been complaining for a long time too, so why can't somebody do something about it?"

His exasperation was penetrating and it struck a chord with me.

So here we were: me, Ann, from a family brought up through the Great Depression by parents (to whom we listened), who never wasted anything; and Kurt, a survivor of World War II in Europe, who had eaten pork from pigs his family raised on their meager kitchen scraps. Waste was unacceptable to both of us; it was not a word we tolerated.

I began to talk to myself silently. I said to 'Me',

"Did he say 'fatten a couple of pigs on thrown-away lunches?"

The other 'Me' said

"Yes, you heard right, and you want to do something about it, don't you?"

Yep, there was little doubt. Immediately something switched my brain to 'on' and like a reflex jerk I said,

"What a concept!!"— right out loud! —in the main hall!

Being a practical person with a full life I needed a very good reason to take on a new project. I needed to know I could give it my all. But I also loved, and still love, unusual, way out, creative, magical things people do to make a difference.

It only took 27 seconds to decide. I walked up to Kurt and excitedly said, "Let's, Kurt! Let us fatten a couple of pigs on those lunches!"

Kurt looked at me, suspiciously at first. Suspicion changed to disbelief. Was someone actually listening to him for a change? Then his tired face began to brighten with amazement and surprise, and he said, "What! Are you serious?" And I said, "Of course. Maybe we can cut down on the wasted food."

It was my high school. But I was a stay-at-home mum, not a student. I loved this school. Sometimes I thought I spent more time at the school than our kids did. I had held just about every executive position on the parent's association and now I was in charge of special events. I wanted it to be the best school in West Van, and thinking up unique ways to promote the school was my job. Raising pigs at the school would fit right into my mandate —unique? —you bet—a very special event.

Then Kurt spoke. He wasn't angry any more. In his usual quiet, considered way he said, yes, he'd lend his moral support to such a project if it could cut down the waste.

I needed to strengthen my case, so I pressed on. "Besides, Kurt, the price of bacon has sky-rocketed. It's over a dollar a pound now. I'm pigheaded about this and refuse to buy it at that price. We've eaten bacon and eggs with our porridge every morning since the babies could eat solid food and we really miss our bacon. Maybe for a while we could bring home the bacon—our own real bacon? We could make this a special event for the school." Now he looked excited too. That's when I got him!

Thinking about it on the way home, I began to see the hurdles we'd have to jump before we could actually make things happen. But first, I took a couple of steps for granted, such as—of course the family would join right in and be part of this, we did everything together. And—of course Tom (he's my husband) would build the pigsty at the school just because he loves building things.

I never thought he might not want to build it. And maybe the kids would say "No!" Also I never thought about where you get pigs; or what would happen when school lunches ran out; or about handling pigs that grow big and heavy and strong; or about us going off sailing in the summer holidays; or…or…. or—ignorance is bliss.

But I did wonder how much help I'd need and who those helpers would be. That was hurdle #1 in my mind. Then—whoops!—would the school actually let us do it?—hurdle #2. Then I remembered that someone had wanted to raise some chickens in West Van recently and had problems with a bylaw. Would pigs be legal in West Van? When you think about it, they don't actually fit the affluent, urban West Vancouver image! Hurdle #3 might prove to be a big problem.

Yes, this was infamous West Vancouver. In 1976 it was well known as home to the Beautiful People, the ones living in the fast lane. We had our share of movie stars, world statesmen, politicians, royalty, and business tycoons, even gangsters, as fodder for society columns, gossip and headlines—those who kept up with the next jillionaire at the country club, on big yachts and at posh parties. They made West Van notorious as a playground for the rich and famous. How was a working pigsty going to fit in here? On the other hand, other types lived in West Van too—ordinary families with ordinary interests like school musicals, soccer and hockey teams, lawn cutting, and doing their own house work. Maybe raising a couple of pigs for a school project would fit into their lifestyle—not glamorous—but intriguing—maybe thought provoking?

I decided to run the idea by my friend, Dave Urquhart, the biology teacher at the school to see if he thought it would be possible. He laughed and said it sounded like fun. After a minute he went on. "Hey! I could have it for a science project. Biology 11 does a section on zoology, so why not?" He figured I'd need a school sponsor for this, then laughed some more and said, "Don't ask anyone else to sponsor this because I want to!"

Hurdle #1 was taken care of already because Dave said the students in the class could earn points toward their final mark if they helped with the Pig Project. By now I'd found out that our family would help too. We had the helpers. This was a great start!

By the next morning I had briefly discussed the idea with Tom and we decided, all things considered, it would be a better plan not to build the pigpen at the school since the likelihood of vandalism loomed large and constant supervision over the premises would be necessary. What would be better than our place? Yes, our home would be the place.

We built our house in 1957 on a sloping lot. Naturally! Most lots sloped on the North Shore. We lived on the side of a mountain! 'Hillside Gougers' was one name they gave us. The front door was on the north or high side of the lot but the back door on the lower part of the lot opened onto a lawn surrounded two gigantic cedar trees with a swing between them. Around the edges you could find a clothes line, a playhouse, a jungle gym, and a bed for a few vegetables, especially for my favourite—tomatoes. The lawn sloped gently down to the lane. All of us in the area, with great difficulty had petitioned the Municipality to build this lane —a lane destined to have a spectacular, though brief, moment in history.

WEST VANCOUVER SECONDARY SCHOOL
OFFICE OF THE PRINCIPAL

March 19, 1976

Mrs. T. P. Barker
1380 Palmerston Ave.
West Vancouver, B.C.

Dear Ann:

I am writing this before our session with
the School Board on Monday night. I know
it will go well, but I want to say it before
we get into a furor. I really appreciate
your support and your 'nuttiness'. It is
really helpful when you know you will get
honest feed back on issues and support
when things aren't going well. Thank you
again for all you have done and are doing
for the school.

Yours sincerely,

R.J. Carter
Principal

RJC/gn

Tom had concrete stairs and a slab already built at the lane for the beginnings of a carport. We had visions of our boys working on cars there in their spare time. We discovered that it might be the perfect place for a pigpen for now, six blocks from school on our own property, about 50 feet from the house, facing into a lane with a shallow ditch for run off. This was exciting! But we didn't have any idea if the space was too big or too small. How much space do pigs need? We'd soon find out

I think we had identified Hurdle #4 with this plan to build the pigs' homesty at our house. What if the neighbours didn't want it there? Oh well, we were getting ahead of ourselves now. We needed to get the OK from the school and the Municipality before worrying about the neighbours.

When we told West Van Secondary's popular principal, Jim Carter, about our plan, he thought I was nutty, but being a good sport and adventuresome, was actually thrilled with the idea and said "Yes! I think it would be really interesting. Let's go for it!" Number 2 Hurdle was a walkover. He had good connections and knew we could get help with swine husbandry from UBC. He got into the spirit of making our plan work from the word "go".

Now, we needed to get the politics straightened out. A delegation consisting of Jim Carter, Dave Urquhart and me needed permission to appear before the West Vancouver Municipal Council in order to give notice of intent to raise a couple of pigs. A simple letter put us on the next meeting's agenda and we showed up. Council, had in the meantime rooted out some by-laws concerning farm animals which decreed it illegal to raise chickens, horses, boa constrictors, cows and/or goats in West Van boundaries. Lo and behold swine were not included! Therefore—would we be OK? Our principal, a man with great charisma and a born salesman to boot, told the Trustees at the meeting that the purpose of the pig project was to demonstrate a concrete alternative to waste (with the possibility of a small profit for a worthy cause), and to raise two pigs on a diet of "high class garbage fit for humans." He told them, "I think it's the first time it's ever been done in a school, and that it is one of the most positive educational innovations in North America." Council was impressed.

Special exemption was voted on and granted by the municipality. To keep swine within city limits was unanimously approved by the Trustees; although one of them quipped they might be saddled with a "pig in a poke!" We were OK. We cleared the third hurdle!

STUDENTS FATTEN UP PORKERS:
Lunch leftovers fit for pigs

By RICH BROWN

Half-eaten peanut butter sandwiches, banana peels and apple cores usually get thrown in the garbage and forgotten about in school lunchrooms. But not so at West Vancouver Secondary School where the edible waste food is carefully sorted and sent to those in need.

No, it's not being sent off to the starving millions in India or wherever. It stays right here in West Vancouver.

It's all part of a biology project at the school. Six students under the guidance of teachers and parents are raising two pigs in order to "focus on waste in the school lunch area, the value of recycling garbage, the profit possible from creative use of waste and the study of pigs by senior biology students."

School principal Jim Carter gave his wholehearted support to the program and presented it to school trustees Monday night, who in turn approved the project, although at least one trustee quipped they might end up saddled with a "pig in a poke."

The two pigs, named Bert and Ernie by students, are being kept at the home of one of the students. Special exemption has been granted by the municipality to keep swine within the city limits. Neighbors were also asked to give their consent.

The pigs are fed about 30 pounds of "food" a day. When they are full-grown by this summer they will probably be butchered.

The idea for the project came from the school's head custodian. He had lamented the throwing away of perfectly good lunches for years and one day made the fateful statement "We could fatten up a couple of pigs with what we throw out each day!"

The only food given to the pigs is from lunches students bring to school. No food from the cafeteria kitchen is allowed to go into the pigs lunches.

Biology teacher Dave Urquhart is in charge of organizing students Paul Greening, Brenda Miller, Karen Halstead, Tom Barker, Chris Bradley and Jane Crickmore as garbage collectors and pig tenders.

It looked as if we were in business. This was going to be fun!

Now was the time to inform all immediate neighbours of our intent and get their permissions to raise hogs in our backyard. Out of the nine families around us, every house except one had school aged kids. I went around to each house and told them what was expected to happen with the project, about pig aroma, and I answered their questions. Whenever I asked the final question—'Would you have any objections?' each said "No, no objections."—even that 'one' house with the older family. They liked the idea. Not one was against it. In fact, the general consensus was "what we did on our property was our business."

What we did on our property was live. We have a family of five. MaryAnn and Jane had already graduated from West Van High; MaryAnn was in 3rd year at UBC and Jane was on her way home after touring Europe as a nanny for our next door neighbour's two little girls. But the other three, John, Kim and Tom Jr., in grades 8, 9 and 11 respectively, were still bringing home all their friends, enjoying all types of action sports with a menagerie of animals adding to the fun and confusion. The kids, along with some parents, practiced musical instruments which the neighbours must have heard. I never heard any complaints.

In the sixties and early seventies, it seemed natural for friends and creatures to come together spontaneously wherever there was space and welcome. Our yard was one of many such gathering spots. One day I counted 50 kids playing on our basketball court in the front yard. We were between dogs just then, but Oboe, Boomer, and JP often came down the street to play doggy games with the humans. Three ducks, Hughy, Dewy and Louey, waddled through occasionally, looking friendly, but they also flew down their driveway when in a frisky mood to attack little children's ankles. Pigs wouldn't do that. At one time, a pair of young goats wandered around pruning anything and everything we planted. Pigs wouldn't do that either. The usual house pets were around—cats, a rabbit and guinea pigs; in fact we always had guinea pigs and always one called

Weelom. Kim earned the lifelong nickname of 'Guinea Pig' from her brother, John, and it was a miracle to me that we didn't have guinea pig trees growing in the garden, from all the little ones that we planted there as they expired.

The fourth hurdle was not a problem. We had nice neighbours. It was such a great place to live and to raise kids. Don't forget those fifty kids in our garden! Things got a little active at times but everyone, parents and children, children and children, parents and parents, were happy to be together.

So the neighbours, after being canvassed were well aware of what was in store for a few months on Palmerston Avenue.

Now that the first four hurdles were cleared, the focus of the Pig Project was perfectly clear:

—the waste in school lunch areas

—the value of recycling "garbage"

—the study of pigs by senior biology students

—the possible profit from creative use of waste

I followed Mr. Carter's suggestion, contacted the Department of Animal Science at UBC and made friends with Aggie Professors, Dr. Dick Beames and Dr. Hugh Saben and the farm manager, Paul Willing. They gave me all the pertinent facts for raising pigs, including the plans and instructions for their pen. They visited the site and said it was perfectly suitable. So the actual pigpen construction by Tom Sr. started, and he built it to those scientific specifications, but also to local building codes which had to allow for stresses involved in snow load and earthquakes! As a structural engineer, he had a good time building it. He was pretty quick, but we, the family, still wanted him to go faster. We couldn't wait to get going.

Half the pen was roofed for the sleeping quarters and the rest was open for the feed trough and room for pigs to move around. Drs. Beames and Saben came to inspect the pen again because now they were responsible for the welfare of these pigs. They passed it with flying colours. They told us we could get piglets from the UBC farm.

Two forty pound wiener pigs would cost about $20 each. Our kids were pretty excited about the whole thing, so when their dad finished the sty, Kim and I took a trip in the little brown station wagon over the Lions Gate Bridge and out to UBC. We brought a pair of very cute two month old piggies home in gunny sacks and introduced them to their new home at Palmerston Ave. This was March 1976 right in the middle of our 29 years of living in West Van.

We were in it for the long term now. Little did I know what special pets pigs could become in just a few months—or that they could turn certain people into vegetarians.

I tried to insist that our children not give names to these animals because I thought there would be less heartbreak when the project ended if they were just numbers. I tried to get the kids to call the pigs by their official numbers—#1022 and #1087—but no way—right away they were Ernie and Bert.

Even though they were both pure white we could tell them apart—Bert's eye pigments were different—one blue and one yellow. Bert was the girl and her face was fatter than Ernie's.

It was decided that the whole thing would be wrapped up at the end of June when the pigs would have to be butchered and the meat sold to the school staff and parents. This would be very hard, I knew, but it had to be thought of as a mini farm situation transferred to the most urbane of urban areas. We would have to suffer what farm families had to suffer when animals went to auction. We had to prepare ourselves for this. We were mentally playing out a few scenarios—a science project; an object lesson; a total recycling project and a Greek tragedy—to make the finale the least traumatic.

Mr. Urquhart's biology students who signed up for the project were Paul Greening, Brenda Miller, Karen Halstead, Tom Barker, Chris Bradley and Jane Crickmore. They would receive points toward their marks for Biology 11 according to the amount of time devoted. The two youngest Barkers were also big players on the team, as they were around all the time and loved these critters that quickly became part of the family.

PIGS EAT LUNCHES STUDENTS THROW AWAY

"TAKE A LUNCH TO PIG" is a special project at West Vancouver secondary school. Pigs Bert and Ernie are being fed with lunches which students throw away. Student garbage collectors and pig tenders are (left to right) Brenda Miller, Jane Crickmore, Paul Greening, Chris Bradley and Kim Barker (see story below).

A notice was sent home to the parents announcing the start of the Pig Project, giving the reasons and hoped for results. If parents knew their home-made lunches were being thrown away perhaps they could talk to their kids about a change. On the other hand, if we managed to reduce the amount of waste and, therefore, partially meet one of our objectives, we would have to find other food for the pigs, because we were committed now, to keep them and fatten them for market.

We would think about that tomorrow.

But then why, you ask, would parents continue to make lunches when they found out what was happening? Well, kids being kids, we suspect they'd say, "Who me? Throw my lunch away? Not me! It must be someone else!" Or else simply, the notice would never make it home. It was obvious to me parents were not succeeding in teaching their families the motherhood issue—"waste not want not." The number of thrown out lunch bags did decrease for a short time, but gradually returned to the previous level.

However—getting back to the pigs......

We started the first day for these toddlers carefully, according to instructions from Dr. Saben. Only two or three cups of food were required and if they lay down without finishing that much, we were to remove the excess. We quickly worked up to the contents of thirty or so unopened lunch bags from the cafeteria garbage cans alone, each day. There were plenty of other cans around the school to raid if we needed more. No food from the cafeteria kitchen was allowed to go into the pig lunches. This was to be the diet for three months. A small supplementation from the grocery department of the local Safeway happened only when absolutely needed on some weekends.

Can you believe it? Kids would drop their unopened lunch bags—full of food prepared with TLC at home—drop them in trash cans at school and then drive down to Marine Drive to eat cholesterol loaded, deep fried, commercial junk food.

We created a roster for the six grade 10 science volunteers who took turns each day going through the cans, picking out the lunch bags, opening, unwrapping and putting the food in a large plastic garbage bag. This is where our amiable janitor, Kurt, gave his moral support to the project. He kept the trash cans scrupulously clean—as he indeed kept the rest of the school—for the sake of the students. He never dealt directly with Ernie and Bert.

The worker of the day then carried the bag with about thirty pounds of food the six blocks to our lane after school. First, they had to slop out the pen. We always watched Karen when she arrived in a pretty dress and gumboots. She turned her head, held her nose and, with one hand raked out the old straw that was fouled by our healthy swine. She was very cute!

"DINER'S DELIGHT

Feeding pigs is a endless job but can be fun. So says Karen Halstead, one of several West Vancouver Secondary School students who earn certificates for supervising such activities. These pigs live in a pen in the yard of the Thomas Barker family, 1380 Palmerston. They were born in December at the University of B.C. and the Barkers obtained them in March. Some food is left-over lunches from the school but most is over-aged vegetables they get from grocery stores."

The dung was flung into a big oil drum which was placed strategically close to the sty. Add water and stir. It turned into the most wonderful nectar for my tomato plants.

Bert and Ernie contributed to my best crop ever!

The feed trough was cleaned, new straw put down, fresh water poured in, then lunch emptied for Ernie and Bert who accompanied the whole procedure with happy squeals, grunts, much snuffling and a little pushing and shoving. Thirty apples and oranges; ham, BLT, cheese, and peanut butter sandwiches; chocolate cake; Nanaimo bar and chocolate chip cookies every day. Think about it —yummy "garbage". They always went for the ham sandwiches first and ate with great gusto. They were such happy little pigs!

We invented a motto —TAKE A LUNCH TO PIG —a decal to put on t-shirts which the kids wore to "work," and on our letter-head. The original Pig Project became the "TAKE A LUNCH TO PIG" project.

Some parents liked this project so much that they donated money to help defray the purchase cost of the pigs and also the t-shirts. Since a piggy bank would be too small, we opened a bank account —a corporate bank account. It was called LUNCHES INPORKERATED!

Every time Tom Sr. came out to the back yard to cut the lawn or otherwise work, he was welcomed enthusiastically with perky ears and snorts, grunts and snuffles. They had good conversations about a lot of things—in pig Latin? who knows —like cutting the lawn and he said the pigs laughed at him for having to do that. They also discussed big sailboats, the weather, ear scratching, curly tails, and sailing, food, growing up, little sailboats and whatever else pigs and men think about.

LUNCHTIME for Bert and Ernie means 30 pounds of delicious nourishing food that students at West Vancouver Senior Secondary School threw away. Mrs. Anne Barker, mother of one of the senior biology students who is studying the pigs' development, graciously dons overalls at feeding time. She insists on referring to them as pigs 1022 and 1067 to avoid becoming attached to them. They will probably be butchered late this summer. (Marilyn FcFayden photo)

There were two lonely Afghan hounds living across the lane. Their working parents left them outside all day. They lay with their heads under their fence facing the pig sty most of the day, watching and listening. You can believe it or not, but they learned to grunt like Ernie and Bert so obviously, they talked about stuff too.

The media caught on to this unique school project and all the lower mainland newspapers wanted stories about the pigs. The headlines were pretty good. Some of them were "Going the whole hog," "Diners' delight," "Project pig gets classy meals," 'Leftovers a waste? Not in a pig's eye," "Lunch leftovers fit for pigs." and "Garbage." But the stories following these headlines were pretty good too because of inaccuracies and imaginative additions to facts. I guess grumpy editors, deadlines and tired reporters make for writing whatever fills up space sometimes.

Reporters lined up at our front door to get interviews! One day one of the evening newspapers, The Vancouver Sun, arranged for an exclusive interview with me. The reporter, Douglas Sagi, arrived at the appointed hour to find another paper's reporter already in line without an appointment. The two got into a shouting match and I had to step in to stop them. Mr. Sagi won but the second scribe was determined and agreed to come back later taking a place at the end of the line-up. As a result, The Sun paper gave us half the front page—a great article and picture —that continued on to half of page 2 as well. The article is reprinted later with its creative journalism, but it does give a good general picture of our situation and enthusiasm.

The local North Shore paper, The Citizen, had numerous articles and pictures throughout the spring and a wonderful cartoon by Aloine who was well known for poking fun at local events. The original drawing was framed and presented to the principal. It hung on his office wall for years. That great paper, The Citizen, kept the populace well informed about TAKE A LUNCH TO PIG as well as Bert and Ernie's progress.

"Amazing how some projects snowball!"

I was interviewed by CBC Radio for that popular Canadian icon, the Farm Broadcast (this was 1976) and the interview was aired right across this big land of ours. A fact: in 1981, Tom took MaryAnn, John, and me to a conference in Halifax. Someone we casually met, when they knew we were from West Van, asked if we knew the lady she had heard about on the Farm Broadcast, who raised the pigs on school lunches!

The Red Cross was very interested and they had a clever cartoonist draw a full page coloured cartoon. With a good write up in their magazine 'Red Cross Youth' this cartoon and article went all *around* the world headed by a quote by the Federal Minister of Agriculture, Eugene Whelan in his green hat. He stated in his inimitable way "Two million people living in Metro Toronto will throw out more than 300,000 tons of food scraps a year. That's 300 pounds (136 kg) of food per person per year." Our project was being used to show how a school, students, and parents were working together to reduce waste, recycle food, and set a good example to the rest of the world. It made us feel so good to have the project recognized for its worth and not just as a kookie kind of joke in funny old West Van.

Red Cross Youth Magazine

Time for a face wash

John and Fenn and Ernie

Three heads are better than one

Ride'm pigboy!

The Vancouver Province was the other evening paper in 1976. Its editor wanted a special story with pictures. The reporter spent the whole afternoon right in the pig pen with Ernie and Bert trying for the perfect shot. Now these were smart pigs! They had soon become sick of looking into the ubiquitous camera lenses. So, on this particular day they went on strike and would not cooperate. They stood in the corner of the pen, curly tails facing out! This poor reporter finally came to the front door around 5 o'clock to admit that he had to leave, defeated, because he had to cover another story—the great violinist, Yehudi Menuhin with the Vancouver Symphony Orchestra at the Orpheum! Because he didn't have time to go home to change and shower, or even use our shower, he hoped I would understand why the symphony picture would be a long distance shot. He didn't think that anyone at the Orpheum would appreciate his eau de cologne de swine!

On the May long weekend when there were no school lunches, we had to improvise, so we hoped MacDonalds might co-operate with a donation of food. We went down to ask for handouts and sure enough they were glad to give us five Big Macs that had landed on the floor and then been put in the garbage. We gratefully accepted them and fed our excited pigs who apparently loved the change in diet until they got king-sized tummy aches! Actually, it looked as if they were dying next morning, because they were lying on their sides, heaving, ears limp and flopped over, asking for help. Some grain that we scraped up that afternoon from the railway tracks by the Saskatchewan Wheat Pool on North Vancouver's waterfront, and lettuce trimmings from Safeway, got us over that weekend. Ernie and Bert recovered. The newspapers wouldn't touch that story!

"The perfect picture of Paul Greening, our model pig tender, with Bert while Ernie hides. Paul was one of the most faithful , who didn't take up agriculture for a career because of memories of smelly piggies."

Another time when we augmented their food with a donation from a restaurant, they also became ill. Pig indigestion is a sad sight.

The kids took the pigs for walks around the neighbourhood, and sometimes through our friends' gardens. Occasionally we had to repair a lawn after Bert and Ernie rooted up the grass with their snouts. Did you know dandelion buds are called swine snouts? Have you ever *really thought* about pigs' snouts? And what wonderful implements they are? The turned-up end, and strength of the snout and neck make it possible for them to cultivate huge fields, to dig up and eat roots, and to hunt for truffles for farmers. They are still used for these jobs on small farm operations.

We didn't want Bert and Ernie to have too much exercise and become slim swine; after all they were being fattened up for a reason. But they were definitely allowed to have their fun and range time with the kids on a pre-arranged schedule. They soon grew too large for the original rope harnesses made to fit 40 pound wieners, so John eventually had to cut the harnesses off, and then they were herded by our pig/men and pig/women, with a stick.

Outdoors Unlittered, a non profit, charitable organization, in the forefront of recycling, ecology and conservation, became interested in TAKE A LUNCH TO PIG after I wrote and requested a bundle of plastic bags which they gave away for an annual anti-litter week campaign. They sent their Information Officer, Patricia Hogg, a reporter and a movie camera man to interview me. With a name like Patricia Hogg, we had some fun on a lovely warm day in May! We expected and got great coverage—a whole page in their monthly "Newslitter" letter.

A project for you?

Going the whole hog

"Bert" and "Ernie"

" Enough food to feed a couple of pigs " How many times does this thought occur when we throw away food waste. Dozens... hundreds ? But what can we do about it you may ask.

The grade 11-12 students of West Vancouver Secondary School have come up with an answer - buy a couple of pigs and recycle it.

With the co-operation of administration, biology department, custodians and parents, they are fattening two pigs, affectionately known as Bert and Ernie, on the wasted lunches that are brought into school.

The scheme has been so successful that teachers and students have formed a Company appropriately named "Lunches InPorkerated" and " Pig Certificates " are issued daily to pupils who feed and clean-out the animals. These will be cashed when the pigs are sold.

Our Information Officer Pamela Hogg looks on as CBC-TV interviews Mrs. Barker (right).

Pigs eat all of left-over lunches everyday. Each weigh nearly 120 lbs.

The idea started when Mr. Kurt Kirmse, custodian at the school realised what amount of food waste was being thrown away. Mr. Kirmse mentioned to the Principal, teachers and the Parent Advisory Committee, that indeed there was enough food waste to fatten a couple of pigs.

Mrs. Ann Barker, a member of the Parent Advisory Committee contacted the University of B.C. and with the go-ahead from the Principal of the school, Bert and Ernie arrived weighing-in at 60 lbs each.

They " live " in Mrs. Barker's back yard and are treated just like ordinary pets. At the moment the pigs are going through between 30-50 lbs. of waste food daily, and weigh nearly 120 lbs.

And what is going to be their fate....Outdoors Unlittered were told that by the middle of the summer they will be ready for marketing, and arrangements will be made to have the meat frozen and packed and returned to school for purchase........ infact a TOTAL RECYCLE.

Time to feed the pigs!

One afternoon I came home from shopping to find all our kids and various friends, a cat, a rabbit, John's iguana, Kim's guinea pigs—and two real pigs in the family room watching TV! I laughed so hard I forgot to take a picture! Not to worry, though, the picture remains forever in my mind. It was funny, fine, and very safe because the pigs had house-trained themselves. They are anything but porcine, in fact are extremely fussy, using a special corner of their pigpen in which to defecate so their sleeping quarters stay clean. It is true what knowledgeable people say, pigs are clean critters.

Our oldest daughter, MaryAnn, came home on the weekends from UBC and walked in via the back lane. She met, John our grade 8 son, more than once, riding Bert down the lane to meet her, like John Wayne on old faithful. Bert always wanted to unseat John, running against the fences, trying to rub him off.

Some of the school helpers disappeared along the way, but Tom Jr., Kim and John were faithful to the end and worked with the pigs every day they could and they grew to love these very neat animals. Kim used to go to visit them and lie in the fresh hay with them! They were not only good buddies to us all, they were also physically and socially healthy! Drs. Saben and Beames checked periodically on their progress, to insure there were no signs of hoof rot or cruelty to animals and that weight gain was right on schedule.

TAKE A LUNCH TO PIG continued with lots of laughs, work and satisfaction through April, May and into June. Ernie and Bert grew, at the required rate, to look like prize hogs, feasting on all the high class West Van "garbage". Some people even thought we should keep them longer and enter them in the PNE in August. That was not in the plan, however.

Graduation day came and Tom, with his friends, Happy Galpin and

Graeme Greene, decided it would be a good idea to have the pigs involved in the school convocation ceremony so they began to get Ernie and Bert ready. It was a very hot June evening and the gym was packed with family and friends, fanning themselves with programs, waiting happily to see their kids, dressed in their best, parade across the stage, shake hands with the principal and get their diplomas. For some, the speeches were long and boring. One couple, who did not seem to be getting along too well that night, and maybe had partied too much beforehand, started an argument that got vociferously out of hand. The school staff took control and unceremoniously ushered them out. More awards were presented and the speeches went on and on. The temperature continued to climb! It was a bit tense in the gym.

Back at the ranch the boys struggled with extreme determination to get the pigs into the car.

It was too far to walk. In the end, they managed to get only Ernie into the back of the little station wagon and I drove them to school. Tom and the boys were graduating the next year so they had planned to advertise their grad early and had decked Ernie out with a Grad '77 sandwich board. Then Ernie didn't want to get out of the car. They struggled and eventually got him to the open door of the gym and held our now, large hog, ready for his graduation walk across the stage. Mr. Crittenden, the vice principal, saw them. From the stage, he suddenly began waving his arms and all but yelled out "Don't come! No! Don't!" The kids got the message! Not a good idea to walk in at that point. So they loaded the pig and reversed the whole procedure back to base. Come to think of it, how might that pig have behaved? What if it had bolted? Could they have controlled a 150 pound Ernie?

The next morning, Saturday, bright and early, principal Jim Carter was on the phone to me to apologize for not allowing Ernie to graduate! He was very sorry, and thought it would have been a great addition on any other grad night—but not that one!

Leftovers a waste? Not in a pig's eye

By DOUGLAS SAGI

Ann Barker is worried that this story about Ernie and Bert, the two pigs she is raising in her back yard, will be just another one of those things that make people laugh at West Vancouver.

"Everyone laughs at West Van," she says. "They call it 'Martini Mountain' and think it is a silly playground. I mean like that guy who launched his 40-foot boat in his swimming pool. Most people in West Van are very ordinary. We're just ordinary."

Ann Barker, her husband, Tom, who is a partner in an engineering company, and their five children live at 1380 Palmerston, a home they call "Barkerville."

It is an ordinary, as Mrs. Barker would describe it, West Vancouver house with a paved front yard where there used to be a lawn. Barker despaired of raising five kids and grass also, so he turned the lawn into a badminton and basketball court.

The back yard is mostly grass and big trees sloping down to the lane where Barker is building a carport. In the place where the carport is being built is a rough

plywood box 10 feet long and eight feet wide. Part of the box has a roof on it, an expensive roof, covered with asphalt shingles.

From inside the box there comes, as one approaches down the slope of the Barkers' back lawn, the unmistakable aroma of pig. Ernie and Bert live in the box.

"The one with the thin face is Ernie," says Mrs. Barker. "The girl is Bert. That's Bert, there, I think. Yep, that's Bert."

There is tumultous activity from deep within the sheltered portion of the box at the sound of Mrs. Barker's voice. Ernie and Bert are 200 pounds each and they crash to the door of the box like a pair of pass-rushing linebackers.

The door is several boards in slots. Mrs. Barker lifts out the two top boards so the pigs can stick their heads out over the bottom boards. Then she gets down on her knees to talk to them. Ernie, the one with the thin face, nibbles at her ear.

"They're so appreciative of any attention you give them," Mrs. Barker says.

ANN BARKER . . . with Bert and Ernie

—George Diack Photo

"Pigs" page 2

THE VANCOUVER SUN: WED., JUNE 23, 1976

Leftovers a waste? Not in a pig's eye

By Douglas Sagi

Ann Barker is worried that this story about Ernie and Bert, the two pigs she is raising in her back yard, will be just another one of those things that make people laugh at West Vancouver.

"Everyone laughs at West Van," she says. "They call it 'Martini Mountain' and think it is a silly playground. I mean like that guy who launched his 40-foot boat in his swimming pool. Most people in West Van are very ordinary. We're just ordinary."

Ann Barker, her husband, Tom, who is a partner in an engineering company, and their five children live at 1380 Palmerston, a home they call "Barkerville."

It is an ordinary, as Mrs. Barker would describe it, West Vancouver house with a paved front yard where there used to be a lawn. Barker despaired of raising five kids and grass also, so he turned the lawn into a badminton and basketball court.

The back yard is mostly grass and big trees sloping down to the lane were Barker is building a carport. In the place where the carport is being built is a rough plywood box 10 feet long and eight feet wide. Part of the box has a roof on it, an expensive roof, covered with asphalt shingles.

From inside the box there comes, as one approaches down the slope of the Barkers' back lawn, the unmistakable aroma of pig. Ernie and Bert live in that box.

"The one with the thin face is Ernie," says Mrs. Barker. "The girl is Bert. That's Bert, there, I think. Yep, that's Bert."

There is tumultuous activity from deep within the sheltered portion of the box at the sound of Mrs. Barker's voice. Ernie and Bert are 200 pounds each and they crash to the door of the box like a pair of pass-rushing linebackers.

The door is several boards in slots. Mrs. Barker lifts out the two top boards so the pigs can stick their heads out over the bottom boards. Then she gets down on her knees to talk to them. Ernie, the one with the thin face, nibbles at her ear.

"They're so appreciative of any attention you give them," Mrs. Barker says.

"They like to be washed and have their place cleaned out. They give me little nips and they have a special little noise for us when we come to talk to them."

Ernie and Bert make their special little noise and Mrs. Barker scratches them both behind their ears.

The pigs are a project of the senior biology class at West Vancouver secondary school. The idea was for the class to raise two piglets by feeding them leftovers from the lunches students brought to school and threw away.

"It was really Kirt's idea. Kirt Kirmse, the janitor. He's from Europe and he would get so furious at the stuff the kids were throwing out. He kept telling them you could fatten half a dozen pigs on the good food they were throwing away. He was disgusted at the waste," says Mrs. Barker.

Ann Barker got involved because she is the public relations person on the school's parent association. If you wonder why West Vancouver secondary has a public relations person you haven't been paying attention.

Anyway, the project was enthusiastically endorsed by principal Jim Carter.

"One of the most positive educational innovations in North America," he told a meeting of West Vancouver's school trustees.

Biology teacher Dave Urquhart organized his class to be pig food collectors and personally constructed the, ah, pig pen, in Barker's backyard.

"I had to phone the municipality and see if it was all right and it was," says Mrs. Barker. "They've got bylaws against keeping goats and cattle and chickens, but there's no swine bylaw." She giggles. "Maybe there'll be one in a couple of months."

The Barkers have marvelous neighbours. Understanding. This is not an editorial comment. It is a fact.

"I telephoned them all and they said it was all right. One man said that anything I wanted to do in my backyard was fine with him," says Mrs. Barker.

One neighbour, owner of two Afghan dogs may be having second thoughts. The dogs have taken to grunting like pigs when they want to be fed. Mrs. Barker says so, anyway, and I believe her.

The Barkers have learned, as do all keepers of pigs, that the animals are instinctively clean. Ernie and Bert are careful with their droppings, depositing them on one corner of their pen, never messing their sleeping quarters.

John Barker, who is 13 and almost as enthusiastic a pig person as his mother, shovels up the manure twice a day, or more often if necessary, and deposits it in a bright yellow reclaimed oil drum, which Mrs. Barker calls her "honey pail." The contents are intended for her tomato plants.

"People in Europe keep pigs this way a lot. It's not at all uncommon. There should be more of it there. Pigs are perfect recyclers," she says.

Daily, one or two of Urquhart's students arrive at the Barker home with the pigs' rations. The food is collected in a barrel in the school lunch room. On a typical day there will be half a dozen whole apples and half a dozen whole oranges, as well as assorted apple cores and other partly eaten fruit. There will be at least 25 whole slices of bread from uneaten sandwiches.

"It is dreadful. If the mothers of those kids knew what they were throwing away. The kids go to McDonald's and leave their lunches in the pig barrel," says Mrs. Barker.

The pigs' diet is being supervised by Dr. Hugh Saben, an animal sciences specialist at the University of B.C. Saben's department sold the pigs to the school last March when each one weighed less than 50 pounds. Ernie cost $48 and Bert, being a girl she was lighter, cost $45.

"They eat anything, but we have to be careful that they don't eat too much meat," says Mrs. Barker. "Boy, do they love ham sandwiches That is total recycling, isn't it?"

Enthusiasm for the project at the school is not as high now as it was when it began and the kids were busy making and selling T-shirts that read "Take a lunch to Pig," but enthusiasm remains high at the Barkers.

"I'd like to see the school do it again next year," says Mrs. Barker. "But we'll have to have younger students. The older ones got tired of it and John and I ended up with all the work.

Not that there is all that much work to raising two pigs. There's the manure to clean up, but that's an easy job if it's done often enough. Ernie and Bert got out once, but they didn't stray far and one of the neighbors telephoned to tell them about. It.

They've become pets, of course. John Barker takes them out for a run up and down the back lane, herding them with a length of rake handle. This is not especially good for pigs that are being raised for food, but Ernie and Bert enjoy the walks and John finds it fun.

Raised for food? Certainly. You didn't think this was just another story about funny old West Van, did you?

The pigs are to be slaughtered the meat and hams cured during the summer. Then it will be auctioned at the September meeting of the West Vancouver secondary school parent advisory committee.

It is an object lesson in the good that can come from half a ton of leftovers. That's right, they've figured it out —1,000 pounds of leftovers make 400 pounds of pig.

They're coming for Ernie and Bert on Thursday.

Eventually, at the end of the term, there were no more lunch bags for Bert and Ernie. A friend at Fletcher Limited volunteered his company to be the place to take them to end the project. The day came and all my friendly helpers disappeared. Either they were busy or they didn't want to be there. Except Kim—she stayed with me as they loaded Ernie and Bert into the truck—with great difficulty. It was a horrible day and we felt so bad for them we cried. However, we had to go through with it and Kim and I stood together holding hands as we watched them drive away.

Bert weighed in at 132 pounds and Ernie at 144. In three months, they had gained a total of 196 pounds because the stress of leaving us would cause them to lose a few pounds.

"**ERNIE**" the pig and his pal "Bert" the pig are ready for the butcher's block. A West Vancouver secondary school project, the two pigs were fed school lunches kids threw away. In three months, the pigs gained 150 pounds each, which meant they ate over half a ton of wasted lunches. Meat from the pigs will be frozen and auctioned at the school next fall.

Here it is: 196 pounds from about half a ton of thrown-away bag lunches, in only 3 months, at only one cafeteria in only one high school— producing first class amazing animals of which to be proud!

The abattoir has an index reading along with the dressed weight that is used for pricing the meat. The index is derived from an adjusted scale and back fat. The index wanted is 100 per hog and if over that, you are paid more than the market weight. We were over the 100, so were paid, that day, $60 /100. If that means anything to you—then good on you! I wanted to have this story as detailed as I could get it. After all, it was partly a science project.

It was a total and complete recycling project too, because after Fletchers dealt with the meat it came back to the school in ham sandwiches the next year. You see, Fletchers froze the spareribs, chops, sausages, feet and neck bones and roasts. The smoked bacon and hams were sold to parents over the summer, because those cuts are better fresh, and LUNCHES INPORKERATED had some early deposits. In the fall, packages of the frozen meat were sold to the parents and teachers who made ham sandwiches for school lunches. Bert and Ernie returned to school in different forms just like butterflies.

We raised $350, which was the final deposit listed in LUNCHES INPORKERATED. Part of this went to the school and part to the *Empty Stocking Fund* at Christmas.

But the story is not quite over because in July that year, the Superintendent of Schools for West Van received a letter from the Regional Veterinarian of Agricultural Canada. Somebody snitched on us! He asked that the project not be repeated. The Vancouver Sun reported it in September.

ONCE UPON A TIME there were two little pigs, Bert and Ernie but these two pigs didn't stay little for very long due to West Van Secondary's generous garbage. Ann Barker donated a portion of her West Vancouver backyard as a home for Bert and Ernie and students from West Van High fattened the twosome with all the good garbage found after every lunch in the cafeteria. But alas this lovable pair had to come under the knife fetching over $350. One hundred of the total goes back to the school to reimburse the purchasing of the pigs, the rest will be donated to a worthy charity by all the students that worked so hard to keep the pigs.

Vancouver Sun. Sept. 10, 1976

Ernie and Bert slops illegal

Ernie and Bert, those two pigs who thrived on the leftover lunches of West Vancouver secondary school last spring, were dining illegally.

The two hogs, 200 pounds each when they were slaughtered in June, shouldn't have been fed raw garbage, according to the federal agriculture department.

The garbage should have been cooked first.

And if the school wants to continue its pig-raising project, it's going to have to get a federal licence.

"Such licences are only granted after certain conditions are met," wrote Dr. H. W. Knapp, regional veterinarian for the department, in a letter to school district superintendent E. M. Carlin.

The meat of Ernie and Bert — the names were supplied by the students who raised them — was tested at the University of B.C.

"It was as good or better than the meat on the pigs the university raises scientifically," said Mrs. Ann Barker, the parent who allowed the pigs to be kept in the back yard of her Palmerston Drive home during the three-month project.

Dr. Ross Marra, regional supervisor of the agriculture department's health of animals branch in Vancouver, said he didn't doubt the meat quality was excellent.

But quality of meat for human consumption isn't the point, he said. It's quality of garbage for pig consumption that troubles the department.

Certain viruses, especially those causing such illnesses as swine vesicular disease and hog cholera, can be found in garbage, Dr. Marra said.

Particularly suspect is pig meat. The viruses are not harmful to humans and could exist in meat taken from an infected animal. The viruses can survive processing and some cooking.

It is possible for a hog to get hog cholera by eating a leftover ham sandwich if the ham came from an infected pig, Dr. Marra said.

Canada has been free of hog cholera since 1962 but there was a serious outbreak in the United States and Puerto Rico in 1972. The disease is devastating to swine herds.

Garbage is a traditional food for pigs, of

"Students" page 2

Students' pig food 'illegal'

Continued from page 1

course, which was why the West Vancouver students began their project.

"It's an excellent project," said Wilf Bennett, chairman of the West Vancouver school board. "The students were recycling food and stopping waste and showing a good example."

The federal r e g u l a t i o n s, Bennett claimed, "are nonsense."

Dr. Marra is sticking by the regulations.

"If we made an exception for them it would set a precedent that would make enforcing the regulations more difficult," he said.

He agrees that the project is a good one and he would like to see it continue.

"The school should get in touch with us. I think something can be worked out," Dr. Marra said.

Licences to feed pigs garbage are usually given only to pig feeding operations that are large enough to have cookers for the garbage and the source of the garbage is carefully watched.

It is also legal for farmers to feed pigs household scraps. The practice becomes illegal when garbage is collected from outside the farm where the pigs are raised.

Bennett said the matter will be discussed at Monday's meeting of the school board.

As for Ernie and Bert, their smoked hams and cured bacon were sold last summer to the teaching staff at the school and $112 was placed in the school's pig fund.

There is another 250 pounds of fresh pork roasts, chops and sausage deep frozen. It is to be auctioned later this month at the first meeting of the Parent-Teacher Association.

We had had vague thoughts of repeating it but conscientious Drs. Knapp and Marra helped to change our minds. We were feeding our pigs "garbage"! Never once did I think West Vancouver food could be considered "garbage". But there *are* government definitions and regulation.

When he said it is possible for a pig to get pig cholera by eating a left over ham sandwich from an infected pig, it made sense. Remember how we observed the pigs first hit on the ham sandwiches at lunchtime?—they loved ham sandwiches and would eat every last one. But when he said the disease is devastating to swine herds as witnessed in the US and Puerto Rico in 1972, I thought this is hardly a herd!

When we realized the West Vancouver School Board chair, Wilf Bennett, said it was an excellent project with students recycling food, stopping waste and showing a good example. He said the federal regulations "were nonsense," we were heartened. And when Dr. Marra agreed the project was a good one and would like to see it continue, it was nice to hear. I for one couldn't find energy to start working something out the Department of Agriculture. The School Board cared a lot and did discuss it again at the next meeting.

Apparently, our project was discussed even in Ottawa, because the Ottawa Journal had an article suggesting we had violated the controversial act pertaining to the feeding of swine and were libel for a fine. Even though it was an educational project, "Unless a permit is first obtained ….no person shall feed swine … or permit swine … to have access to or to be fed any raw or cooked garbage composed of meat, scraps, offal, kitchen waste, fruit or vegetable refuse ….. which has been obtained elsewhere than on the premises where feeding takes place….." We must have slipped through the cracks!

Anyway, been there, done that! We didn't pursue the matter any farther and we completed our project, tying up all the loose ends by December.

An affluent society begets more waste than a poor society. This waste was graphically demonstrated by West Vancouver Secondary School thirty years ago. How far have we come in our thinking in thirty years? Is there less wasted food in 2007?

Probably not. However, I believe in our part of the world there is more awareness about recycling, about not wasting and about working together to reduce the waste and pollution. Now, if we do our best and allow this energy to ripple out into the greater picture, there will be an effect on others. It only takes a little shift in frequency to affect all other frequencies.

At any rate, we completed our project. We did not reduce the waste significantly then, but we did recycle food, we did try to stop waste, we did learn something about swine, and we did show a good example. If it made even a few people think and let them know that they, themselves, could do something to help their communities and themselves, then TAKE A LUNCH TO PIG did succeed.

And it was fun!

And all the females in our family became vegetarians.

And I decided someday I'd write a book about it.

And this is it!

THE END

APPENDIX:
Hog raising by Dr. Beames and Dr. Saben

The breed of our pigs was York Land Race Cross.

When we bought them from UBC they were 2 month old wieners of about 40 lb.

The market price was $ .70 per lb.

They sold pigs for 1/2 the market price to 30 lbs. then $.15 up to 40 lbs.= approximately $20 per pig.

On day 1 wieners require 2 —3 cups of food. If they didn't finish that much and lay down , then they'd had enough. Remove the rest.

Pigs weighing 40 lbs. require 2 lbs. of dry matter per day,

8 lbs. if there is 50% moisture.

When pigs are approaching market weight they need up to 14 lbs. per day.

They also require 2 —3 gals. of water per day.

In 3 months they should be between 160 and 220 lbs. live weight.

This means they gain 1 —1 ½ lbs. per day.

3 lbs. of feed = 1 lb. of weight gain.

When they reach 65 —70lbs. they could go without feed on Sunday.

They will consume approximately 600 lbs. of feed to market weight.

We were to report regularly on their weight gain:

place a tape measure around the body at the front legs and phone UBC to report.

BUILDING AND CARE OF A PIG PEN

50 sq. ft. required per pig; but 1 pig at 200 lbs requires 6' x 10'
6' x 6' would be OK for us
4' high fence for sides
4' x 5' box with a low insulated roof for pigs to be sheltered inside
The extra 2' is for an outside run
Need straw in the box in which to burrow and sleep
Need a wooden platform off the ground

Droppings in the straw to be trenched each day
Wash the urine down each day

The last time the by-law was re-written in West Vancouver in 2002, it was made illegal to raise any live stock except a horse or miniature horse, and only in special areas.

Printed in the United States
by Baker & Taylor Publisher Services